Extreme Couponing For Busy Women

A Busy Woman's Guide to Extreme Couponing

HowExpert Press & Brandy Morrow

Copyright HowExpert.com

COPYRIGHT, LEGAL NOTICE AND DISCLAIMER:

Table of Contents

Introduction

Today, around 50 percent of all consumers regularly use coupons when shopping and 49 percent of adults over the age of 18 have used coupons in the past 30 days, collectively saving about 800 million dollars each year! The average value of each coupon used is about $1.50. Today, coupons are available for almost every single product that you can buy and couponing is becoming more and more popular by the day.

Where there was once a time when an extreme couponer would be the one and only couponer in their city, now, even in small towns, there are multiple couponers in search of the best deals to save them money.

The savings can be amazing when you use coupons for the items that you purchase. There are those who simply aim to save 50 percent on everything that they purchase, while others will not purchase anything that they cannot get for at least 80 percent off after coupon.

So why isn't everyone couponing? The answer is time. We have all been led to believe that if we want to be an effective extreme couponer, we have to devote at least 40 hours a week to couponing and treat it like a full-time job. While most of us already have full-time jobs, as well as families to take care of, homes to run, meetings to attend, and bills to pay, we simply do not have 40 or more hours per week to devote to couponing.

The good news is that if you coupon effectively, no matter how busy you are, you do have enough time. You do not have to spend 40 hours a week, clipping coupons, searching for deals, and shopping because much of the work is already done for you.

Throughout this book, I am going to teach you exactly how you can coupon no matter how busy your schedule, so that you no longer have to pay full price for all of the items that you purchase.

Why Coupon?

Using coupons when you purchase your groceries or other household items is a great way to save money. Imagine that someone has handed you a 500-dollar check. Would you feel comfortable taking that check and throwing it in the trash? Of course, you wouldn't. Instead, you would take that check, deposit it in the bank, pay your bills, or purchase something that you need.

Coupons are basically free money that the companies are giving you. Each company allocates a specific amount of money each year to use to attract more customers to their products. Some of the money that is allocated to attracting customers is distributed to consumers in the form of coupons. Not using the coupons is basically throwing money away.

The average consumer that uses coupons randomly, or when they find a coupon for something they like will save about 30 dollars per week, which adds up to 1560 per year! However, the average extreme couponer is going to save a lot more.

Many people refuse to use coupons because they are simply too embarrassed. They are afraid that by using coupons, they will look poor or cheap, however, according to recent statistics, those who have an annual income of 100 thousand dollars or more are twice as likely to use coupons regularly than those families that have a lower income.

Why? The reason that people are using coupons is not so much about the money that they will save during one shopping trip, but instead, it is about how much they will save over a specific amount of time.

If your family currently spends 150 dollars per week on groceries as well as household supplies, (which is a very conservative amount) and by using coupons, you are able to save 50 percent, you are freeing up 75 dollars each week to invest or pay toward your mortgage or to put into your savings account. What if you save 60, 75, or 80 percent on your grocery bill? How much could you put into a savings account? What could you do with that extra money?

Too Busy Isn't an Excuse

Today, we don't have to spend hours upon hours looking for the best deals or planning out our shopping trips because we have all of that information right at the tip of our fingers. You can go as far as never clipping a coupon but instead adding them to your shopper's reward card if that is offered at your grocery store.

The bottom line is that couponing is a great way to save tons of money, but the mindset will spread into the rest of your life as well and you are going to find that you are focused on saving as much as you can on every purchase you make. On top of that, it is just fun! You get to watch your total at the register go from 300 dollars to 60 dollars, people gasp, they are amazed at what you are doing, and you walk out of that store with your head held high because you have learned an amazing skill.

Chapter 1 - Getting Started

The first thing that you need to do when you are getting ready to start using coupons, is to change your mindset. You are going to be changing the way that you have been shopping and opening your mind to something that can change your life.

You are no longer going to be making runs to the grocery store between shopping trips. There will no longer to be huge shopping lists that do not take price into account or shopping without a plan. You are not going to be creating your weekly meal plan without first knowing what you are going to purchase. You are going to stop going to the wholesale clubs making huge purchases.

Instead, you are going to start planning your meals around what is on sale and what you have coupons for. You are going to start saving between 50 to 90 percent on all of the grocery and household items that you purchase. You are also going to start purchasing items when they are on and when you have a coupon for them, stocking up when the items are free or almost free.

Let me tell you a story about the types of deals you can expect to get. I can only use a certain brand of shampoo and conditioner. It is the only brand that does not irritate my scalp. Each bottle of the shampoo and conditioner that I use is 5 dollars, which means that I used to pay 10 dollars per week for 1 bottle of each.

Now that I use coupons, I pay 49 cents per bottle and I stock up for 6 weeks, meaning that I purchase enough of that shampoo and conditioner to last me until the next sale. For the 6 weeks, I need 6 bottles of shampoo and 6 bottles of conditioner, which means that I spend about 6 bucks when I stock up. Now, instead of paying 60 dollars for shampoo and conditioner during those 6 weeks, I am saving the 54 dollars and putting the money toward something else. That is just one item. Imagine how much you could save if you use coupons on multiple items.

Start Collecting Coupons

After you have gotten into the right mindset and are ready to start saving money, you have to start collecting coupons. I am asked on a regular basis where I get all of my coupons and the answer is very simple. Everywhere.

Once you start couponing, you will start seeing coupons everywhere you go. The absolute best place for you to find coupons is in your local newspaper. You will find in your local paper that there ones are called inserts. The inserts that you may find in the Sunday paper are Procter & Gamble as well as the Smart Source. There is a third insert that many people get in the mail on Wednesdays called the Red Plum, however, if you do not receive this in the mail it can be found in your local paper with the other inserts.

In order to start extreme couponing, you will want to get your hands on these inserts. I suggest that you purchase one paper for each member of your family. What this will do is ensure that you are able to purchase multiples of the items that you need and each member of your family will have one.

Therefore, if you have a family of four, make sure you are purchasing four newspapers each Sunday.

The next way that you can get coupons is to use Internet printable coupons. There are many different places that you can find printable coupons, from coupons.com to manufacturer's Facebook pages. What is great about these is that they are free, however, you can only print 2 identical coupons per device.

Of course, you are going to have to have a device as well as a printer and you will have to download coupon printing software, however, this is safe software that is used by hundreds of thousands of people every day.

There are also mobile coupons. This is one of the fastest and easiest ways for you to coupon. These coupons are on your cell phone. Some of them include Cartwheel, Checkout 51, and Ibotta. We will talk more about these apps later on in the book.

eCoupons are also available at different retailers, they are also known as digital coupons. These are loaded to your loyalty card or to your phone number that is associated with your loyalty account. Once you add them to your card or account, they will automatically come off at the register when you swipe your card or enter your phone number.

There are peelies, which are found on the products that you are purchasing in the store as well as Blinkies that are found in the aisle, next to the product. When you pull out a blinkie, another one spits out.

Finally, there are store coupons that can be found on the bottom of your receipts. Make sure that you are watching out for these because if you just throw your receipt away, you could be missing out on some great deals. For example, one store offers 5 dollars off of a purchase of 25 dollars or more on the weekends. You may have to take a survey to get a store coupon but they are worth watching for because they can reduce out of pocket costs dramatically.

There is also coupon clipping services online that you can use to get your coupons. This service is a bit controversial at the time because the coupons specifically state that they cannot be sold, however, the coupon clipping services state that you are not buying the coupons, instead, you are paying them for their time.

Time to Get Organized

You have the right mindset, you have the coupons, now it is time to get organized. The way that you organize your coupons can make or break you. There are a few different ways that you can organize your coupons, or you can come up with a way of your own.

If you are wanting to save as much time as possible and only purchase the items that you know you are going to use, you can use the File Method.

In order to use the File Method, you are going to need a box, file folders or tabs, and your coupons. Each week when you purchase your newspapers, you are going to take the inserts out and place them into a folder for that week. You will place each type of insert into its own folder, and then label the folder with the name of the insert (Smart Source, Red Plum, or Proctor & Gamble) as well as the date that the insert came out.

This will make it easier for you to find the coupons when you need them for your deals. For example, if you find on the coupon matchups that Silk Effects is on sale and there is a coupon in the June 18th Smart Source, all you have to do is find that insert in your file box and clip your coupon.

If you are a bit more of an extreme couponer or have a deep need to be organized, you may find the binder method easier for you to use. This is the method that I prefer because I am able to find my coupons quickly, and if there is an unadvertised deal, I don't miss it since all of my coupons are in my binder, right there with me.

In order to create a couponing binder, you will first need a binder and you will need baseball card holders. You will want to organize your coupons by category, for example, hair products, bathroom products, office products, and so on.

This method is going to take a bit more time, however, as long as you keep up with clipping your coupons and placing them in your binder each week, it will only take a few extra minutes. Each week after I purchase my coupons, I will sort the inserts, staple them together so that I only have to clip them once instead of multiple times, then after they are clipped it takes me about 10 to 15 minutes to organize them all in my binder.

The savings that I get from this is insane. While someone who does not clip all of their coupons is going to be able to get the deals that they know about, I am able to get deals that put my savings over the top. What I mean by this is that when I get to the store, if I find an item on clearance for example, and I know I have a coupon for it, I can get the item for free or almost free instead of hoping that I get back with my coupons before someone else gets the deal.

I also find that this helps me when I have to put deals together on the fly. This may happen if you find that a certain item that you were planning on purchasing is not in stock, but you need to reach a specific dollar amount in order to redeem a store coupon.

For example, if I go into a store with a store coupon for 5 dollars off of a purchase of 25 dollars or more and only take the coupons with me that I am planning on using if I find that an item I was planning on purchasing is out of stock, I have two choices.

The first choice is to walk away and not get any of the items and the second choice is to go ahead and purchase items that I do not have a coupon for which will take away from my savings. Taking my binder with me ensures that I can put deals together, even when stores are out of specific products that I have coupons for.

Collecting your coupons is going to take some time. You will want to have at least three weeks' worth of coupons before you ever set foot in the store, but the good news is that as you collect your coupons, you can learn everything that you need to know about couponing. This will ensure that when you walk into a store, you are confident that you know what you are doing and that you are using your coupons properly.

Chapter 2 - Learning Coupon Lingo

In order to ensure that you are using your coupons properly and to understand the information that is posted on coupon matchup websites, you have to understand the terminology that is used on coupons as well as couponing lingo.

Understanding this information is going to ensure that when you do finally get into the stores you know what you are doing. This is important because as you will soon find out, there are a lot of cashiers out there that do not understand coupons and you may find yourself explaining the proper usage to them.

Lingo

BOGO- this simply means Buy one, get one and it is usually followed by the words free or half off. BOGO free, also written as B1G1, simply means that if you buy one product, you will get a second product for free. BOGO half off means that if you purchase one product, you will get the second product for 50 percent off. You may also see B2G1 or another version of this. It simply means that if you purchase 2 items you will get one free.

Blinkie- A term I used in the previous chapter, it refers to coupons that are put out by manufacturers in the aisles next to the products that they can be used on and are dispensed from coupon machines. They are called blinkies because they usually have a red blinking light on them. The blinkies will come out of the dispenser one at a time and you do not have to redeem them in the store that you find them in. In other words, you can save your blinkies and use them for a better deal because they are not store coupons but are manufacturer coupons.

Catalina- Also referred to as a CAT, these are coupon machines which are located at the cash register. You will receive these coupons with your receipt after you have paid for your purchase and they can be used at on your future purchases. The Catalinas can be store coupons or manufacturer coupons. If the Catalina is a store coupon, it can only be used at the store, you received it from, however, if it is a manufacturer coupon it can be used anywhere that accepts coupons.

Insert or Coupon Insert- This is another term that I used in the previous chapter and it refers to the circulars that are found in the Sunday papers. The coupon inserts, which can be found on a regular basis include, Smart Source, Red Plum, and Proctor & Gamble, although all three are not found every week.

PG- This is the Proctor & Gamble insert, it usually comes out once per month.

SS- This is the Smart Source insert and comes out several times a month.

RP- This is the Red Plum insert and comes out several times each month.

Couponer- This is another term that I have already used and one that you are going to see a lot in this book. It is also a word that you should get used to being called because it describes a person that uses coupons to save money on the products that they purchase.

Double Coupons- There are a few, and I do mean a few, stores that are still doubling coupons, however, it is usually only up to a certain value. For example, the local store where I live will double coupons up to .50 this means that when I go in with a coupon that is .50 cents or less, they will double the value of the coupon, making it 1 dollar or whatever the value is doubled. However, if I go into the store and use a coupon that has a value of. 51 cents, I will only get .51 cents off of the product, there will be no doubling.

There are also a few stores that double coupons on a certain day of the week, so make sure that you check with your local store to find out if they do offer doubling, what they will double up to, and if it is offered on a certain day of the week.

eCoupons- We spoke a bit about this earlier when we were talking about where you can get your coupons from. The eCoupons are coupons that you will load onto your store card and that will be taken off of your total when you swipe your card or type in your phone number.

ECBs or Extra Bucks- If you are speaking to a couponer who has been couponing for a while, they may talk about ECBs. Txhese are now known as Extra Bucks and are part of a rewards program at CVS pharmacies. These will print on the bottom of your receipt and can be used just like cash. You will get these when you make a purchase that qualifies. In order to find out what type of purchase qualifies you will want to check your local ad or your coupon matchup sites.

EXP- This means expiration date. You cannot use your coupons after the expiration date unless you are in the military and using them at the base store or if your store policy allows it.

Handling Fee- There is small print on the bottom of the coupon where you will see that the company, which is accepting the coupons, will receive a handling fee for each coupon on top of the value of the coupon from the manufacturer. This means that the manufacturer is going to reimburse the company for the value of the coupon as well as the handling fee, which is about 8 cents per coupon. (This is important to know because you may get told you are stealing from certain stores that do not understand how coupons work, you can then explain to them that they are reimbursed the value of the coupon and 8 cents per coupon, then walk out of the store with your head held high.)

MIR- This means Mail-In Rebate; which means that in order to get a rebate you must submit the rebate by mail, usually with a proof of purchase such as a receipt. These are simply traditional rebates and after receiving your proof of purchase, the manufacturer will send you a check for a certain amount.

Manufacturer Coupon- These are coupons that are put out by manufacturers in order to expose more consumers to their products. These coupons can be used at any store that accepts coupons. When the store redeems the coupon, the manufacturer is going to reimburse the store the full value of the coupon as well as the handling fee.

One Coupon Per Purchase- This means that you, as the consumer, can use one coupon per item that you are purchasing. This also means that you cannot use two manufacturer coupons on the same item.

One Coupon Per Transaction- This comes in many varieties, you can find coupons that state, two coupons per transaction, four coupons per transaction, and there are coupons that do not limit the number you can use per transaction. This simply means that you can only use that specific number of coupons in each transaction that you have. However, this is not going to stop you from doing separate transactions. For example, if you have 4 coupons that state you can use one coupon per transaction, you can do four different transactions in order to use your coupons and get your products.

One Coupon Per Day- This is a limit that is getting more and more popular, of course, you may also find coupons that state, two coupons per day, or four coupons per day. This means that you cannot do separate transactions, but that you are only going to be able to use your limit for that day in that specific store. There are people who do not agree with the fact that you can go to a different store but that is the reality. If you have 8 coupons that state you can only use 4 per day, you can go to two stores on the same day and use all of your coupons.

The previous three terms are very important for you to remember because when certain cashiers start looking at your coupons, they tend to confuse per purchase and per transaction, you need to be able to explain to them what it means.

Peelie-I also used this term when I was talking about the different ways that you can get coupons. These are manufacturer coupons that are found on the products that you are purchasing in the store. These are usually good on products besides the ones that you find them stuck to however, you need to make sure that you are reading the fine print when it comes to the Peelie to ensure that you can use them on a different product or on a smaller sized product.

Raincheck- There are going to be times when you go into your store to get a deal and find that they are sold out. That is when you go to customer service and ask for a rain check. These are slips of paper that state that you can get the item for the sale price when the item is restocked, even if the sale is over. The store may include a limit or an expiration date on the rain check.

Rolling Catalinas- This is something that you will hear often if you shop at a store such as Kroger, which usually has some type of Catalina printing out. When a Catalina is rolling it means that you are going to separate your purchase into several transactions in order to use your Catalina on your next purchase. Once you use the Cataline, another will print out. This is called rolling.

In other words, let's say that you are at Kroger and the Pine Sol is on sale for 99 cents, however, when you purchase 5 you get a three dollar Catalina that is rolling, and you want to purchase 15. In order to lower your out of pocket, you will purchase the first five, pay the 5 dollars and get the Catalina for 3 dollars. On the second transaction, you will purchase 5, use your Catalina, and pay 2 dollars out of pocket. Another Catalina will print out and you can keep this going as long as you want.

OOP or Out of Pocket- This is the amount of money that you actually pay out of your pocket. This is, after all discounts, coupons, ECBs, and Catalinas are taken off of your total. If you are following a coupon group on social media, you will often see a post with a picture of items and it will say something like: Retail-196.83 OOP-21.35

This simply means that the person paid $21.35 out of their pocket for all of the items that they purchased.

Stacking, Coupon Stacking, or Stacking Coupons- This means that you are stacking two promotions. You may be stacking a coupon with a sale or you may be stacking a manufacturer coupon with a store coupon (which is completely acceptable) however, you can NEVER stack a manufacturer coupon with a manufacturer coupon.

Stockpile- This word can have a couple of meanings. To stockpile means that you are purchasing items that you are going to put into your stockpile. Your stockpile is the area that you store the items that you have couponed for. When you purchase items on sale and with a coupon, you will be purchasing multiples, you can create a huge stockpile or just use a closet in your house, but you are doing this so that when you are out of an item, such as shampoo, all you have to do is go to your stockpile and get a new one. This ensures that you never run out of anything that you need and you NEVER have to pay full price.

Store Coupon- This is a coupon that is put out by the store in order to entice you to purchase the product from that specific store. Stores are not reimbursed for their own coupons and these coupons can be found at the bottom of your receipts, in their weekly ads, online, or downloaded eCoupons.

Loyalty Card- This is a card that your store offers you which, when presented at the checkout will provide you with additional savings. You can also download coupons to your store loyalty cards. If you do not have a physical card, you can use your phone number to get the same deals.

Transaction- This refers to each time that you pay. I can purchase 50 items in one transaction.

Purchase- Each item that you are buying is a separate purchase.

WYB- This means When You Buy. On some coupon matchup sites, you will see this. For example, Buy 2 Garnier Shampoo or Conditioner at 2.49 each, use 1 $4/2 coupon, Final Price, .49 cents each WYB (when you buy) 2.

$1/2, $2/2, $4/2- You will find coupons that are going to give you a discount if you purchase a specific number of items. When you see this on your coupon matchups, the first number is going to be the dollar

value that the coupon is for and the second number is going to be the number of items that you must purchase in order to use the coupon.

Chapter 3 - How to Find the Deals

Now that you know what types of coupons are available, you have your binder set up, and you have studied the lingos, you are probably asking yourself how you are supposed to know where all of the deals are.

First, you need to determine what store you are going to coupon at. When you are first starting out, I suggest that you decide on learning how to coupon at one store in order to reduce confusion. After you have mastered one store, you can add in another and so on.

There are a couple of different ways for you to find the best deals. You can, of course, use the store flyers, which can be physical flyers, or you can find them online. Of course, since you are busy and don't have a lot of time, this may not be the best option for you.

The second option is to use coupon matchups sites. When you are searching for a coupon matchup site, you will want to go to your search engine and type in "the name of your store" coupon matchups.

You are then going to find a huge list of all of the different matchup sites. I do suggest that you give the top three sites a chance. Some people will find that they prefer one site over another. "Bookmark" to save the sites you like the best for future reference.

What you are going to find on these sites is that the owner of the site has already done the work. Let's say, for example, you want to learn how to coupon at Dollar General to start off with (which I highly suggest), you will type "Dollar General Coupon Matchups" into your search engine and find the site that you like the most. Basically, you are just going to decide based off of the way that the site is set up because the sites are all going to have the same information. You will find that some sites are just easier to use than others.

As you go through the list of the matchups, you will see the name of the product, the sale price, the coupon to use on the product as well as what insert the coupon can be found in, and the expiration date of the coupon. Next, you will see a breakdown of how to use the coupon for example:

Tide Pods- 2.95, use $2/1, June 4 P&G, exp. 7-1

Purchase 4 Tide pods, use 4 $2/1, pay $3.80 plus tax OOP or .95 each

What this says is that you are going to purchase 4 packs of the Tide pods at $2.95 each and use the $2/1 coupon that came in the June 4th Proctor & Gamble insert. You will end up paying $3.80 plus tax for all 4 packs of Tide pods which means that they are going to end up being .95 cents each.

All that you have to do as you are going through the coupon matchup site is decide what deals you are going to do.

Once you do this, you have two options, you can write the deals down on a sheet of paper or you can checkmark the deals on the website or blog and print the list out. No matter how you do it, knowing what deals you want to take advantage of is going to help you create your shopping plan.

It is important that you keep track of these deals because this is where a lot of people spend the majority of their time. Because you are pressed for time but still want to save money by using coupons, it is vital that you only have to visit the deals once so that you can start planning out your trip.

Before we go further, I want to take a minute to talk about the shopping trip. This is where a ton of people end up spending a lot of time as well because they feel that they have to hit every store and get every deal. If you do this, you are going to be wasting your time, your gas, and your money.

Not every deal is a good deal. Not every deal needs to be gotten and the fact is, you are going to miss out on some deals no matter how hard you try not to. The good news is that these deals come around again and again so if you don't get it this time, you can get the deal next time.

Pick one store and I do mean one store. If you want to start saving on household items, and choose Dollar General, start by going to ONE Dollar General a week. Once you are comfortable, you can then add other Dollar Generals or other stores.

This is not a race to see who can accumulate the most stuff. When you are first starting out, get what you need in multiples. Worry about creating a stockpile if that is what you want later on.

When it comes to finding out about the deals, we all know that some deals are unadvertised, however, if you are on social media, you can follow a group that specializes in the store that you are couponing at. What is great about these groups is that they will post the unadvertised deals as well as different scenarios that you can use in your store to save the most money.

Take some time to think about the store that you are going to be shopping at. Do you want to start with food items or are you going to save more if you start out by couponing for household items? What are your local stores?

Now go familiarize yourself with some of the coupon matchup sites for that store. Jump on social media and find a great group to follow so that you are always up to date on the best deals.

Chapter 4 - Rebate Apps

While rebate apps are not technically coupons, many couponers use these apps on top of their coupons in order to save even more, or to save money on items that we do not regularly get coupons for

Most of us have heard of rebates, they have been around for what seems like forever. Years ago, our grandparents would use tons of mail in rebates to get money back on their purchases but now we have rebate apps which will allow us to save a bit of money.

You can download the rebate apps on your Android or on your iPhone and use them to earn cash back every time you shop. The great thing about these apps is that you will get the rebate even if you use coupons on the item.

How Do They Work?

The first thing that you will do is to download the app on your smartphone. The most commonly used apps that you can search for are Ibotta, Checkout 51, Mobisave, and Savings Star.

The next step is to go on your shopping trip. When you are using these types of apps or when you are couponing, in general, you will want to save your receipt. After you have finished your shopping trip and have a few moments, you will open the app, take a picture of your receipt using the app, and then submit your receipt.

After your receipt is submitted, it will be reviewed to verify that you did purchase qualifying items and if you have, cash will be added to your account. You can request a check, direct deposit, or a PayPal payment, depending on the app that you are using.

There are also other apps you can submit your receipt to including: ReceiptHog, Walmart Savings Catcher (only for Walmart receipts) and ReceiptPal to earn even more. When you use these apps, you can earn points used to get free gift cards or cash deposited into your PayPal account.

The great thing about these apps is that you can submit one receipt to all of them and earn a good amount of money back on all of your purchases.

Ibotta and Check Out 51 are most people's favorites because they are very easy to use. When you use Ibotta, you will have to unlock the deals before you can claim them, sometimes you have to watch an ad or just click on the icon to unlock the deal.

What is great about Ibotta is that it lists all of the deals for different stores and you are able to get cash back on items that you usually do not get coupons for such as fresh fruit, vegetables, milk, and meat.

The downside to these apps is that you can only claim the deals once (however, sometimes they do increase the number of times that you can claim the deals). For example, if you have 20 cents off any fruit purchase and you purchase 5 separate pieces of fruit, you will only get 20 cents back. The good news, however, is that you will be accumulating money by using these apps, they only take a few seconds, and can be used in your spare time, and you can use the money for items that you want or need.

Chapter 5 - Store by Store

Congratulations for making it this far in the book! If you are not confused yet, get ready to be. Just kidding. Actually, this part is not very confusing at all if you are focusing on learning one store.

In this chapter, I am going to go through several common stores that couponers visit and talk about how you can save the most money at these stores. I do suggest that you focus on the store that you want to start couponing at if it is listed. If the store that you are going to be couponing at is not listed, I suggest that you choose one store from the list that is similar to your store, or simply use one store to help you understand a bit more about couponing.

If you do go ahead and read about couponing at all of the stores I am going to go over, it is likely that you will get confused and it could actually hurt your chances of being a successful couponer.

Before we go into the different stores, there is something that you need to make sure that you have with you at all times: The store coupon policy. Personally, I keep the store coupon policies in my binder in a plastic sleeve so that I am able to pull it out when needed.

It is important for you to understand, couponing is not for the meek. If you are going to coupon, you are going to have to make sure that you are able to stand your ground, that when you are confident that you are doing the right thing, you stand up for yourself, and you never let anyone make you feel bad about saving money.

I like to think of it like this...

While someone wants to make you feel bad about using a coupon, you are getting an item for 50 cents while they are paying 5 dollars for the same item. You tell me who should feel poorly about their decisions.

You are also going to have to understand that cashiers are usually not trained well when it comes to coupons. They will tell you that you can't use a coupon for a specific item, that you have to use the coupon on the item in the picture, or that you can only use one coupon per transaction because they don't know the difference between a transaction and purchase. It is your job to educate them but to do so in a polite and calm manner.

It is very easy to lose your cool when you are couponing and a cashier refuses to take your coupons, however, you cannot do this. If all else fails, if the cashier refuses to listen to what you are saying or refuses to let you use the coupons that you know are right, simply pick up your coupons and walk out the door.

There are, however, going to be times when your coupons just won't scan and this is not the cashier's fault. There are stores that because of the increase in fraudulent coupons being created, will not let the cashiers override the register and key in the coupons. If this happens, offer to put the item back, take your coupon, and continue on with your transaction.

Dollar General

This is one of my absolute favorite stores to coupon at because you can always get so many deals and because you can save a ton of money.

The first thing that you need to know about couponing at Dollar General is to take a look at the bottom of your receipt. Here you will find a $3/15 coupon, which is printable if you take a quick survey. If you have a printer, take the survey because if you don't, you are just throwing 3 dollars in the trash.

There is also another coupon, one that does not have to be printed. It is usually a $5/25 coupon or a $5/30 coupon which can be used on one day of the weekend. On occasion, the coupon will be good for a Monday or for the entire weekend.

This coupon means that you are going to get 5 dollars off of your purchase of 25 dollars or more BEFORE coupons. That BEFORE is very important because once again, there are going to be cashiers that are going to tell you that this is not going to work, that you will not be able to use the $5/25 with coupons, however, they are wrong.

I have been doing this for years, and every time a cashier tells me this, I just smile and say, "Well, scan it anyway because I heard it would work." Of course, it works every time.

Your goal when you are creating a scenario for Dollar General is to create a scenario that adds up to exactly 25 dollars or a few cents over 25 dollars before tax. You want to get your total before tax as close to 25 dollars as you can, this way the 5-dollar coupon is going to take off a larger percentage of your total.

It is vital when you are shopping at Dollar General that you read the coupon and adhere to the requirements. Many people tend to use coupons "because it scans." If a coupon states that it is supposed to be used for a specific product of a specific size, but scans for another product, DO NOT USE IT on the product it was not intended for.

You see, you are going to be couponing with these same cashiers for a while, if they accept a coupon for an item that it is not intended for, they do not get reimbursed for the value of the coupon and you are going to earn a reputation. Instead, be an honest couponer and earn their respect.

After you have created your scenario and you have all of your items in your cart, you are going to want to get your coupons ready. You will want to have your $5/25 coupon as well as your manufacturer coupons. I will say that Dollar General does offer digital coupons as well, but I do not find that they are reliable. Often times, the system is down or the coupons do not come off of the total. If the coupons do not come off, there is nothing the cashier can do to fix it. Therefore, I prefer paper coupons when shopping at Dollar General.

After the cashier has rung you up, she will tell you your total. You need to make sure that it is 25 dollars before tax and if it is, hand her your 5 dollars off coupon. After she rings up this coupon, you will hand her your manufacturer coupons.

If you hand her the manufacturer coupons first or if you let her scan them as she is ringing the items up, the 5 dollars is not going to come off because your total will no longer be above 25 dollars.

If you are using digital coupons, you need to let your cashier know. Tell her not to hit the total button until you have entered your number. You will enter your number as she is scanning the items that you have purchased. All of your digital coupons will come off when she presses total. Then, if you are using paper coupons you will hand those to her.

There is a digital $5/25 coupon that you can use each week and I find that if I am going to use digitals, it is much easier to use that 5 dollar coupon instead of a paper coupon then digital coupons and then more paper coupons. Remember, you don't only want to make this as simple as you can for you, but for the cashier as well.

After the cashier scans all of the coupons, they will give you your new total and you will be amazed!

Dollar General also has 50 percent off clearance events where everything in the store that is already on clearance is discounted an additional 50 percent. On top of this, you are able to use your coupons, which means that you can walk out of that store with an entire cart of products for almost nothing. It is during these sales that it is a good idea to stock up. Because these sales only happen a few times a year, I do go to every Dollar General in my area to ensure I am able to get all of the best deals. That is the one time that I will go to multiple Dollar Generals.

CVS

CVS is a favorite of many couponers even though most people who do not use coupons at CVS will tell you that it is very expensive to shop at. The reason that couponers love CVS so much is that it is actually possible to shop for free at CVS!

CVS offers what is called Extra Bucks deals, they are great when it comes to giving out rain checks, and they have a wonderful coupon machine which prints out coupons that can be stacked with your manufacturer coupons in order to save you even more money.

The first thing that you will need to do is to sign up for an Extracare card at CVS.com or in the store. Often times, you will receive a great coupon such as $4/20 just for signing up online. You will be asked if you want to be part of the beauty club as well and I highly suggest that you take advantage of this. The Extracare card is not going to cost you any money, nor is being part of the beauty club; and it is going to save you huge amounts!

Whenever you make a purchase at CVS, the cashier is going to scan your card which will ensure that you get all of the discounted prices, but even more importantly, it is going to allow you to take advantage of the Extra Bucks deals. This is a very important card and you need to make sure that you do not lose it.

What are Extra Bucks?

These are coupons that are going to print out when you check out and they are going to be located on the bottom of your receipt. They print out when you make a qualifying purchase, which you will find in your weekly flyer or on your coupon matchup site. This is how Extra Bucks deals are usually written out on a coupon matchup site

Buy 2 Garnier Shampoo or Conditioner, $3.00 each

Buy 2 Receive $3.00 Extrabucks, Limit 3

Use 2 $2/1 Garnier Shampoo or Conditioner from SS 10/5

Pay $2.00, receive $3.00 Extra Bucks

Final Price, $1.00 MM

Now let me clarify what MM means. This means that this deal is a money maker. In other words, you are paying 2 dollars out of pocket, but you are getting 3 dollars back. There is a way to lower your out of pocket even more, but I will talk about that in a moment.

For this deal, you can see that the Garnier shampoo and conditioner is 3 dollars per bottle. You have to purchase 2 bottles in order to receive 3 dollars in Extra Bucks on the bottom of your receipt. In order to make this deal better, you will use manufacturer coupons that are 2 dollars off of each bottle bringing your total out of pocket down to 2 dollars for 2 bottles of the shampoo and conditioner. Even though you have used the manufacturer coupons, you are going to get the 3 dollars in Extra Bucks.

As you can see, this also states that there is a limit of 3. That means that you can do this deal 3 times during the week's sale. Even if you go to different CVS stores, you will only be able to do this deal three times. This is tracked at the bottom of your receipt. Therefore, if you do not know how many times you can do the deal again, just look at your receipt.

CVS runs these types of promotions every week and each week they are on different items. One week you may find that the Extra Care deals are on candy, the next it may be on cleaning supplies, and the next it could be hair products. The great thing about CVS is that they do not only run one of these promotions at a time, but instead run multiples.

It is through these Extra Bucks that you will be able to shop at CVS for free. This is called rolling Extra Bucks. You are able to use your Extra Bucks at CVS just like cash to pay for any item that you want to purchase. You can use them to lower your out of pocket and often times walk out of the store paying NOTHING!

Let's go back to the deal on Garnier. Let's imagine that you already had some Extra Bucks, 5 for example.

You want to do the deal three times so that you get your limit and the great thing about CVS is that you can do them all in one transaction. You do not have to split them up in order to earn the Extra Bucks.

So, you would purchase 6 Garnier at 3 dollars each, making your total 18 dollars. Then you would use 6 $2/1 manufacturer coupons bring your total down to 6 dollars. Since you already have 5 dollars in Extra Bucks, you will give them to the cashier making your total 1 dollar.

At the end of your receipt, you are going to get back 9 dollars in Extra Bucks that you can use on the next transaction or save for the following week.

It is important to remember that when you are using your Extra Bucks, that you forfeit any overage. For example, if your total is $1.50 and you give the cashier a 2-dollar Extra Buck, you will lose 50 cents. Be very careful not to waste your Extra Bucks.

One rule that I use when I am using my Extra Bucks is that I never use more than I will get back. In other words, if I have a transaction that I know I will get 20 dollars in Extra Bucks back on, I will use my coupons and no more than 20 dollars in Extra Bucks, and then I will pay whatever little bit is left with cash. This ensures that you always have the Extra Bucks to pay with instead of paying those larger sums OOP.

CVS Coupon Center

The CVS Coupon Center, often referred to by couponers as the Magic Coupon Machine is going to be located inside of your CVS store. Not only are you able to get coupons from the machine, but it works as a price scanner as well just in case you need to double check a sale.

Before you begin any shopping trip, you want to make sure that you go to this machine and scan your card. In fact, don't just scan it once. Scan your card until the machine tells you that you are a super scanner. Doing this is going to not only get you more coupons right then, but it will get you more coupons in the future as well.

When you follow a CVS coupon matchup site or Facebook group, they will post about the types of coupons that are printing, however, coupons vary by person so you might get the coupons you have read about and you might get something else.

The great thing about this machine is that the coupons that print are for items that you regularly purchase. For example, if you regularly purchase diapers at CVS, you will get diaper coupons. On the other hand, if you have never purchased diapers at CVS, you will not get any diaper coupons. This is great because we don't end up with a bunch of useless coupons for items that we do not purchase.

Rain Checks At CVS

CVS has a great rain check policy. If you go into purchase a product that was part of one of the Extra Bucks deals and it is out of stock, just let your your cashier know and they will write a rain check for you. This means that the next time the product is available in the store, you will not only get the sale price, but they will print the Extra Bucks for you as well.

CVS rain checks do not expire and you can stack your manufacturer coupons as well as your store coupons with the rain check to ensure you are getting the best deal. If the Extracare promotion had a limit, this will be written on the rain check, which means that you cannot purchase more than the limit that was advertised when using the rain check.

Beauty Club

One of my favorite ways to earn rewards at CVS is through the Beauty Club. When you are part of the beauty club, you will earn 5 dollars in Extra Bucks for every 50 dollars that you spend (before coupons) on beauty items. These Extra Bucks can be used to purchase any item in the store just like any other Extra Buck. On top of this, you will receive 3 dollars in Extra Bucks each year on your birthday!

The great thing about this club is that you are going to be purchasing beauty products anyway. The products that qualify include hair care, skin care, fragrances, cosmetics, and pretty much anything that has to do with beauty. You are going to be purchasing these items when they are free or almost free and since the beauty club uses your before coupon total, 50 dollars is not hard to reach.

App Coupons

You can also save money at CVS by using their coupons that are on their app. Simply download the CVS app on your phone and sign into your account. Connect your account with your card and CVS is going to start sending you tons of coupons that you can use when you are checking out. These coupons are found under "My Deals & Rewards" on the app.

CVS is an amazing store to coupon at and for those that are a little afraid of rude cashiers, CVS is the place to go. No matter what store I go to, no matter how many confusing transactions I do, the CVS cashiers are the best. They are always willing to go the extra mile to help you and to make sure that you get the best deals.

Kroger

When it comes to grocery stores, Kroger is a favorite for most couponers because they have amazing sales. Many people believe that Kroger is expensive because if you go into a Kroger and purchase whatever items you want, you are going to spend quite a bit. On the other hand, if you pay attention to the sales and use your coupons you are going to be able to save a ton on your grocery bill.

Kroger Card

The first thing that you are going to want to do is to sign up for a Kroger Card. You can get one of these at the customer service desk or sign up for one online. It is important that you use this card every time that you shop at Kroger, otherwise, you will not get the advertised sale prices.

There are some Kroger stores that allow you to earn points that you can use to get discounts on your gas. For each 100 dollars you spend on groceries, you will earn 100 points or 10 cents off of each gallon of gas that you purchase. However, there are some stores that do not offer this so make sure that you check with your store to find out if they do.

Coupons

When you are using coupons at Kroger, you need to make sure that you know the policy. It states that you cannot use more than 5 like coupons per day. However, if you are friendly with the cashiers, they will often let you use 5 like coupons per transaction. This is all up to the manager and your cashier.

Kroger also accepts eCoupons that are loaded directly onto your Kroger card via their website or app. Often times, you will find that these coupons are good for up to 5 uses which is wonderful because most eCoupons can only be used on one item. When you purchase an item that you have an eCoupon for, the value of the coupon is going to be automatically deducted at the register.

Remember that since the eCoupons are manufacturer coupons, you can only use the eCoupon or a paper coupon, they cannot be combined, but don't worry, if you accidentally give the cashier a coupon for an item that you have an eCoupon for, the register will reject the paper coupon.

Kroger Sales

This is the absolute best part of shopping at Kroger. Each month, Kroger has what they call "Mega Events" and often times will have 10/$10 sales. When you stack your coupons with the Mega Event sales price, you are going to find some amazing deals.

One thing that confuses many people is that they believe when there is a Mega Event such as a Buy 5 Save 5 event, they must buy 5 of each item but this is not true. You do have to purchase 5 participating items in order to get the discount but they can all be completely different items. You can buy 30 different items as long as they are all participating items and get the sale as long as you are purchasing your participating items in multiples of 5.

In other words, if you buy 9 items, you are only going to get the Mega Event price on 5 of them. However, if you go ahead and buy 10, you will get the Mega Event price on all of them.

It is during these Mega Events that I tend to really stock up on a lot of products because the deals are just amazing. This is where I get my shampoo and conditioner for 49 cents a bottle as well as so many other products.

Kroger Clearance

Another amazing thing about Kroger is the clearance items and the manager markdowns. When an item is on clearance, you can stack a coupon on the clearance price and often get the product for free or almost free.

The manager markdowns are great for getting items that you don't normally have coupons for, such as meat, baked goods, or dairy products. It is important to check the expiration dates and inspect the product, but as long as you are not purchasing spoiled items, you are going to see huge savings here as well!

Kroger has some of the most amazing sales I have ever seen and if you really want to get the most for your dollar, you will use coupons when shopping there. Maybe you have shopped at Kroger before and thought they were a bit too expensive. If you have, give them another try, but this time, walk in there with your coupons and a plan.

There are some great couponing matchup sites for Kroger so don't feel overwhelmed when it comes to Mega Events and sales. The coupon matchup sites will give you a complete list of the items included in the

Mega Event as well as the coupons that you can use for the items.

What About the Rest

There are so many different stores that you can shop at using coupons and save a ton of money, the ones listed in this chapter are the stores that I have personally found to be the easiest to coupon at, which is important if you want to save money when you have a busy schedule.

Of course, you can start out shopping at any store that you would like. Just make sure that you have a copy of the coupon policy and that you walk into the store with a plan. The truth is that many people believe couponing is some type of science that is difficult to learn when it really is not. Couponing is nothing more than replacing the cash that you would normally spend on groceries and household items with little slips of paper that the manufacturers put out to be used on their products.

Chapter 6 - Couponing Tips To Save Money

One of the biggest challenges that we face as busy women is managing our time. You may love the idea of couponing but then look at your to-do list and wonder how you could possibly fit more in.

Most of us feel this way at some point or another in our lives and it is the number one reason that most people do not coupon. The reality is that couponing is not going to make your life more challenging. The way that you go about couponing is going to determine if it is a challenge for you or not.

Not too long ago, I felt the same way. How could I as a busy woman, taking care of my family, running my home, and running a business ever find the time to coupon? Then I realized I didn't have the time to not coupon.

The first thing that you have to do before you even start couponing is to determine the value of your time. For example, for each hour that I put into couponing, I must save at least 30 dollars. This means that if I put 3 hours per week into couponing, I cannot accept any savings of less than 90 dollars. That is the value of my time. The great news is that I save a lot more than that!

The second thing that you will want to look at is what you actually have to do each day. Many people find that when they look at what they have to do each day as well as what they are actually doing, a lot of time is being wasted.

What could you do instead of spending an hour playing social media games? Could you look for deals? Clip coupons? Make a trip to a store?

It is very important that you take a look at how you are spending your time because while you may think you are being productive, you may not really be.

A Few Tips to Get You Started

1. Clip or file your coupons when you get them. If you are purchasing Sunday papers, do not let the coupons pile up, but instead, clip them or file them as soon as you get home. I like to do this in the evening time when everyone is settling down and watching television.

2. Use the time that you have. What I mean by this is that if you are sitting in the doctor's office waiting for an appointment or waiting for your child to get out of dance class, start searching for deals and creating your list or clip your coupons.

3. Do not spend more than 20 dollars per week on items that are going to go into your stockpile. If you do not put a limit on the dollar amount that you can spend on your stockpile each week, you are going to end up spending too much, couponing is not going to really save you much money, and your stockpile is going to become overwhelmingly huge. The idea is to simply ensure that you don't run out of anything.

4. Only stockpile items that you know you will use. I remember when I first started out, there was a great deal on denture cream. I have no use for denture cream, but it was free so I bought it. That denture cream sat in my stockpile for months before I actually found someone that needed it. If you absolutely must grab those types of deals, do so, but donate what you can't use.

5. Plan your trips for when you are already out. Coming home from church? Stop by the store and grab your deals. Whenever you are already out, double up on what you are doing so that you make the most of your time.

6. Make sure you determine how much time you want to put into couponing. One great thing about determining the amount of time that you want to put into something is that you will usually get done what you need to in that amount of time. If you want to put in 5 hours a week, plan for that. If you want to put in 3 hours a week, plan for that.

7. Don't worry about missing a deal. So, you have 20 bottles of shampoo in your stockpile, but there is a deal that will get you 20 more for free. Let it go. If you can't get the deal it is not the end of the world, the deal will come around again and you can focus on using the 20 bottles you already have.

8. Let other people do the challenging work. You don't have to spend your time searching for the best deals when there are coupon matchup sites out there that do all of the work for you. Couponing really has never been easier. You can find scenarios already written up,

for you online so that you don't even have to make a plan, it is already done.

9. Enjoy yourself. Couponing can be so much fun. It can be exciting, thrilling, but it can be exhausting if you let it be. Remind yourself that this is something that you can enjoy, especially if you love shopping. Don't allow it to become another stressor in your life. If it does, take some time off and just use up what you already have in your stockpile.

10. Don't feel like you have to do it all. I love to coupon for household items. The reason is because that is where I spend a large chunk of my budget. Therefore, my focus is on saving money on household items. I do not really spend a lot of my time focusing on couponing for food, although I will do about 1 large grocery haul a month. I know where I can save the most money and that is where I focus. When I do have a large stockpile of household items, I will take a few weeks and switch my focus to saving on actual food products because, at that point, the food items are going to save me more money than adding more to my stockpile would.

It is all about balance. I heard a saying once: "A person will find the time to do the things that they value." This really hit home for me because I work very hard for the money that I earn and I do value it. I had to ask myself why I would continue to pay full price for items that I knew I could get for pennies if I really valued my time and my money.

Conclusion

While many people know that they can save a ton of money by using coupons to pay for the items that they purchase on a regular basis, they continue to stray away from the idea because they feel that they do not have enough time.

We have allowed other people to convince us that because they spend 40 hours per week searching for ALL of the deals and clipping thousands of coupons, if we are going to coupon we must do the same thing. The truth is, couponing should fit into your life.

It does not matter if you spend 2 hours a week on couponing and another person spends 32 hours as long as you are saving money and that is all that matters.

One of the greatest things about couponing is that as you learn the process, you will become more efficient. You will learn the sales cycles and you will have a general idea of what sales are coming up depending on what coupons are coming out.

The most wonderful thing about couponing is that even if you are saving minimal amounts of money for example, 30 percent off of the products that you buy you are actually saving a ton. If you spend 100 dollars a week on groceries and you start saving 30 percent just by spending a few hours a week clipping coupons and looking up deals, you are saving 30 dollars every week! That is 1680 dollars per year in savings!

Couponing is great for those that are struggling to make ends meet, for those are making ends meet but have little to no money left over after the bills are paid, for those that have some money left, and even for those that do not have any money concerns whatsoever because a dollar is still worth a dollar.

So many people are working two jobs today. We have households where both parents have to work and the children spend their day at daycare. What would you do if I told you that by learning how to coupon, you could actually save enough money to quit one of those jobs or to stay home with your kids or to just cut back on the number of hours that you have to work each week?

That is exactly what couponing will allow you to do. Couponing is going to allow you to start saving for that vacation that you always wanted to take, allow you to purchase those Christmas presents that your kids keep asking for, and allow you to do all sorts of other activities that there just was not enough money for before.

It is going to take some time, everything that is worth doing does take some time, but it does not have to take all of your time and what you will find once you begin seeing savings is that those few hours are worth giving up for the insane amount of savings that you will be getting.

About the Expert

Brandy Morrow is a busy mother of three who runs her own freelance business while still ensuring that her house runs properly, ensures that every meal is prepared at home using healthy ingredients, works out one hour each day and finds the time to coupon in order to save as much as she can. Brandy started couponing 4 years ago when her interest was peaked by the Extreme Couponing show on TLC. Brandy is a self-taught couponer who is passionate about teaching other people how to save money by using coupons. Brandy believes that when we focus on saving the money we earn, we have a huge impact on our own quality of life. Brandy regularly donated items that she purchases with coupons as well as helps out local families that are in need with care packages. Brandy believes that if she can do it, you can too.

Recommended Resources

www.HowExpert.com - HowExpert publishes short 'how to' guides in unique topics by everyday experts who want to share their passion, knowledge, and expertise with the world and make a positive impact in their sphere of influence!

www.HowExpert.com/writers - Write for HowExpert!

www.HowExpert.com/couponing - Recommended resource for extreme couponers.

3 1333 04782 2307

9 781548 478704